# Curious Cases

Plays by Sarah Shillam
and Cath Howe

Illustrated by Simon Cooper

CONTENTS

**Pearson Australia**
(a division of Pearson Australia Group Pty Ltd)
707 Collins Street, Melbourne, Victoria 3008
PO Box 23360, Melbourne, Victoria 8012
www.pearson.com.au



Text by Sarah Shillam and Cath Howe
Illustrated by Simon Cooper, The Organisation
Designed by Sara Rafferty

First published 2013 by Pearson Education Limited.
This edition first published 2016 by Pearson Australia Group Pty Ltd by arrangement with Pearson Education Limited. 

2019 2018 2017 2016
10 9 8 7 6 5 4 3 2 1



ISBN 978 1 4886 1245 9

Pearson Australia Group Pty Ltd ABN 40 004 245 943

Printed in Australia by SOS Print+Media Group

# Curious Case: Life on Earth?

Written by Sarah Shillam

## Characters

**Farmer Joe** – from Planet Earth

**Phobos** – a Martian astronaut

**Deimos** – a Martian astronaut

**Constella** – a TV presenter

**Zorbit** – a TV presenter

**TV producer**

**Daisy the Cow** (non-speaking)

*A breakfast TV show on Mars. Two presenters are interviewing a pair of Martian astronauts about their recent trip to discover if there is life on Earth. A TV producer comments from behind the scenes. Also on the sofa with the astronauts is a pair of Earthlings: Farmer Joe and his cow, Daisy. The Martians ignore everything that Farmer Joe says.*

**TV producer:** Lights! Camera! Action!

**Constella:** Good morning everyone! You are watching 'Breakfast Mars'.

**Zorbit:** Today we will be talking to two astronauts who have just returned from a very special mission. And they have brought along a couple of unusual guests of their own ...

**Farmer Joe:** Hey, Daisy! We're on TV!

**Constella:** We're talking about the expedition that has got all of Mars buzzing – the voyage to discover if there is life on Earth!

**Zorbit:** For centuries it was thought that the blue and green planet was just a pretty bauble on the intergalactic tree …

**Constella:** But our astronauts had a theory that there may be more to this sphere than meets the eye.

**TV producer:** One of the earthlings is drooling! Can we have a tissue?

**Farmer Joe:** Daisy, you must behave! If you mess up the studio we'll get into trouble!

**Constella:** What raised your suspicions, astronauts?

**Phobos:** Well, as you mentioned, we have ignored Planet Earth up until now. From a distance it appeared to consist mostly of water ...

**Deimos:** We Martians don't use much water, so there was never any incentive to look at Earth more closely.

**Phobos:** Then we made a discovery on our last trip to Mercury. As we were travelling through space, something hit our windscreen.

**TV producer:** The Earthling is drooling again. Can we have another tissue?

**Farmer Joe:** No, Daisy, don't eat it!

**Zorbit:** What hit the windscreen?

**Deimos:** It was a plastic box with writing on it.

**Phobos:** That was our first clue. None of the planets we have explored so far use plain old writing any more. Everyone uses holograms these days.

**Deimos:** The object seemed to have come from a planet far behind our own in technology.

**Phobos:** Inside the box were two triangular pieces of bread with something soft and yellow in between.

**Farmer Joe:** Daisy, don't nibble the Martian's ear. It's not polite ...

Phobos: In the old days, we used to believe the Martian moons were made of this yellow stuff. It was called "cheese".

**Deimos:** Cheese was supposedly a delicacy in the Martian prehistoric age, but our historians weren't sure if it actually existed or if it was just a myth.

**Phobos:** It got us thinking about Earth being blue and green. Of course, to get green you need blue and **yellow**, so that meant that there had to be yellow stuff on Planet Earth somewhere ...

**Constella:** So you decided that cheese was the missing link? How clever!

**Farmer Joe:** No, Daisy. Don't eat the Martian's toes, either! I know they look like dandelion leaves but try to behave!

**TV producer:** Zorbit and Constella, please speed things up a bit. We don't have all day on this story. You still have to interview The Lunar Tics ...

**Zorbit:** So you made an expedition to Earth. What did you find when you arrived?

**Deimos:** The first thing we noticed was that it was very green. There was vegetation everywhere and odd buildings with strange machinery inside.

**Farmer Joe:** You landed on my farm!

**Phobos:** Then we spotted some native Earthlings.

**Deimos:** They generally seemed to have four legs ...

**Farmer Joe:** Not all of us ...

**Deimos:** And some of them had little horns on their head. Most of them produced white stuff. This was very important ...

**Farmer Joe:** The white stuff has a name. It's called **milk** ...

**Phobos:** The white stuff appears to be where the planet gets its yellow from. It comes out white but we carried out tests on it and found that, by a simple chemical process, it is possible to turn the white stuff into cheese!

**TV producer:** Presenters, you are running out of time! The Lunar Tics are warming up in the next studio ...

**Constella:** So what's happening next in the Earth Exploratory Programme?

**Deimos:** Well, based on our initial expedition, we don't think that the major life forms on Earth are very intelligent. They simply eat, make "moo" sounds and produce white stuff.

**Farmer Joe:** Why is no one interested in me? Humans are the major life forms on Earth, aren't they?

**Phobos:** But we did bring a couple of Earthlings back with us to carry out some more tests.

**TV producer:** Can we get a close-up of the Earthlings?

**Farmer Joe:** Watch where you put that hoof down, Daisy ... ouch! My toe!

**Zorbit:** I'm sure the viewers will agree that these Earthlings are very peculiar creatures!

**Farmer Joe:** Well that's not very nice! You're a bit weird-looking yourself!

**Deimos:** We're hoping to turn Earth into a cheese-production zone. We think we may be able to use it to give tennis balls extra bounce in the gravity-challenged galaxies.

**Constella:** Well, we look forward to hearing how you progress with your project. Now it's time for us to move on to our next guests.

**Zorbit:** They're at the top of the stellar charts this week with their latest song, 'Supernova'!

**Constella:** Ladies and gentlemen, please give a round of applause to The Lunar Tics!

**TV producer:** Can someone please move the Earthlings? One of them just plopped something brown and nasty-smelling on my studio floor ...

# Curious Case: An Egg-straordinary Event

Written by Cath Howe

## Characters

**Dr Reynolds**
the family doctor with a nose for a tricky case

**Rami**
a soccer-playing boy who is no early bird in the morning

**Mum**
cool, calm and usually unflappable

**Dad** (Dave)
a bit of a worrier and easily beaten

**Gran**
short-sighted and hard of hearing, but a wise old owl

**Dina**
Rami's sister, who has a 'fowl' sense of humour!

**Scene 1**

**Dr Reynolds:** I'm Doctor Reynolds from the surgery on Feather Lane. I saw a case earlier this week that was quite extraordinary – or perhaps I should say 'eggs-traordinary'! Let me introduce you to the Peckton family. Their son, Rami, just didn't get out of bed one morning. That's how it all began ...

*Mum, Dad, Gran and Dina are in the kitchen. Rami calls down from his bedroom.*

**Rami:** Mum!

**Mum:** Get up, Rami! I expect you down these stairs before I've counted to …

**Gran:** You must be firm with him!

**Dad:** Come on, son, you heard Mum.

**Rami:** That's just it – I can't!

**Dina:** Rami is late for breakfast again! I'm not late, am I, Mum? I'm on time. Look, I've got my cereal.

**Gran:** That boy gets away with everything!

**Mum:** That boy! What's the matter with you, Rami? I'm not coming upstairs. Dave, will you go and see him?

*Dad goes upstairs.*

**Dad:** Why is it always me? Now then, Rami, I've had just about enough of your ...

*He gasps.*

**Rami:** Something's happened in the night, Dad.

**Dad:** Everyone! Come quick!

**Gran:** Has he run away?

**Dina:** No, Gran. He's just being really, really naughty!

*Mum, Dina and Gran go upstairs.*

**Mum:** Rami, I … What on earth? Your feet! I've never seen anything like it. Your feet!

**Gran:** What's the matter with his feet? They look perfectly normal to me.

**Dina:** Gran, they're completely the wrong colour.

**Mum:** And shape.

**Rami:** And size.

**All:** And they're scaly!

*Dina looks closer.*

**Dina:** With fluffy bits.

**Mum:** Oh my goodness! This is terrible.

**Rami:** Calm down, everyone. Maybe it's just ... an allergy or something.

**Mum:** Sorry, love, sorry. You're quite right. Dr Reynolds will sort it out. Of course she will. I'll ring the surgery.

## Scene 2

*Later, at the doctor's surgery.*

**Dr Reynolds:** Hello, hello. Come in. Oh my word – the whole family. Come on in. Just perch anywhere. Well now, Rami, how can I help?

**Rami:** It's my feet, Doctor.

**Mum:** Yes, Doctor Reynolds.

**Dad:** We're very concerned.

**Dr Reynolds:** Oh yes, they do look a bit swollen.

**Rami:** They've completely changed!

**Dr Reynolds:** Well now, I do agree with you. They do look rather ... different.

**Rami:** Rather **different**? They don't seem to be my feet at all!

**Dina:** And they have claws. Look!

**Gran:** You never said he had claws. No one told me about the claws.

**Dr Reynolds:** Mmm. Most unusual.

**Rami:** What's the matter with me?

**Dr Reynolds:** Well …

**Dad:** Come on, Doc. Give it to us straight.

**Dr Reynolds:** I'd say, on balance, and obviously we'd need some tests to be really certain, but, just from first impressions, I'd say you're turning into a chicken.

**Family:** What?

**Dr Reynolds:** Now, don't be alarmed.

*Dr Reynolds takes Rami's temperature.*

**Gran:** What do you mean, "Don't be alarmed"? You can't just tell a boy he's turning into a chicken!

**Rami:** I'm on the school soccer team. I can't play like this!

**Dina:** How long will it take? Will he have to live in the shed? Can I have his bedroom?

**Mum:** My little boy – a chicken!

**Dr Reynolds:** The fluff will drop off fairly soon. It shows us you are newly hatched. Tell me, when did this ... begin?

**Rami:** I just woke up this morning and there they were.

**Dr Reynolds:** No pain? No odd tingling? Tell me, have you had any contact with chickens recently?

**Rami:** No.

**Dad:** Hang on a minute – you did have chicken for dinner last night.

**Dr Reynolds:** Ah well, I suppose that could be significant. Nuggets?

*Dr Reynolds tests Rami's reflexes and is kicked by Rami's new foot.*

**Rami:** No, chicken pie.

**Mum:** We all did. I made it. Are you saying it was my pie that did it?

**Dr Reynolds:** Mrs Peckton, please calm down. I'm only asking a few simple questions. Do you eat a lot of chicken, Rami?

**Rami:** No, no, not really. Doctor, it's just my feet. The rest of me is all right, isn't it?

**Dr Reynolds:** Ah, but in cases of this kind it's usually the feet that lead the way, so to speak. How does your face feel? It's just that we would normally expect a beak in the next couple of days.

**Dina:** Rami is going to have a beak!

**Rami:** Have you seen a case like mine before?

**Dr Reynolds:** A couple of dogs. The occasional rabbit. You are, in fact, the first chicken.

**Mum:** That's quite special then, dear. You're her first chicken. You should be proud.

**Dr Reynolds:** Would you mind if I looked down your throat?

**Rami:** No, of course. Take a **cluuuck**! I mean a look – sorry!

**Mum:** Can't anything be done?

**Dad:** It's the Cup Final on Saturday. He's the best striker on the team!

**Gran:** He's not going to be much of a runner with those feet!

**Dr Reynolds:** I'm afraid these cases are usually irreversible. Your best bet is to switch to a diet of corn and kitchen scraps.

**Dina:** Yippee! I get all the biscuits and ice cream and lemonade and cake and jelly and ...

**Dr Reynolds:** And this soccer match ... tricky! You may find your footwork is clumsy but, once you have developed more fully into a chicken, you may be able to flap in the faces of the other team and put them off.

**Rami:** So that's it, then?

**Dad:** I understand how you feel, believe me. Having a chicken in the family is a **fowl** stroke of bad luck! Ha ha ha!

**Mum:** It's no laughing matter.

**Gran:** It's a good joke, though!

**Dina:** It's just bad **cluck**!

**Dr Reynolds:** Think of it like a rare case of chickenpox.

**Family:** Huh?

**Dr Reynolds:** Except, without the pox!

*The family all groan.*

**Dr Reynolds:** Don't get in a flap.

**Rami:** It's going to be okay, everyone. Honestly, I feel fine.

**Mum:** Come on then, chicken. Let's get you home!

**Gran:** Well, there is one good thing, you know.

**Dad:** What's that?

**Gran:** Well, chickens get up early every day, don't they? You won't have to drag Rami out of bed any more.

**Rami:** COCK-A-DOODLE -DOO!